WHERE DID THE SUN GO?

BY   EVELYN AVSHARIAN

ILLUSTRATED BY   SANDY FINKEL

FALLING WATER PRESS

ANN ARBOR, MICHIGAN

Copyright © 1984 by Falling Water Press. All Rights Reserved. Printed in the United States of America.
This book may be ordered directly from the publisher; please include 50 cents postage. We suggest you try your bookstore first.
Falling Water Press, P.O. Box 4554, Ann Arbor, Michigan 48106.

ISBN: 0-932229-01-8

TO THE MEMORY OF EVELYN

WHERE DO THE LEAVES GO WHEN THEY DIE?

LEAVES TURN RED AND GOLD AND BROWN
LEAVES SAIL AWAY FROM THEIR TREES

ON A WONDERFUL WINTER WIND...

PLAYING HIDE AND SEEK UNDER THE SNOW

TILL WARM RAIN AND BRIGHT SUN

HELP THEM NESTLE INTO THE EARTH.

WHERE DO THE FLOWERS GO WHEN THEY DIE?

THE PETALS OF A ROSE BLOSSOM

LIKE SWEET MELTING WINGS

FLOAT TO THE FEET OF ITS PLANT.

WHERE DOES THE GRASS GO WHEN IT DIES?

GRASS CHANGES COLORS.
SEE IT IN THE FIELD THERE, SO LONG AND DRY...?
 IT BECOMES A CRADLE FOR BABY DEER

 AND SOFT GREY RABBITS.

MOTHER AND FATHER BIRDS WILL CARRY SOME AWAY
TO HELP MAKE THEIR NEST.

IT WILL BE A HIGHWAY FOR THE BUSY ANTS...

A STEADY RUG FOR NEW PLANTS
TO GROW FROM IN THE SPRING.

IN THE VERY SAME SPOT
FOR A DAY AND A NIGHT…

OUR BIG EARTH, LIKE A BALL,
TURNS AROUND AND IT'S DARK.

BUT THE EARTH STILL KEEPS TURNING
TILL IT COMES BACK AGAIN
TO THE VERY SAME SPOT

SO WE'RE ALL WARM AND SUNNY.

OPEN YOUR HAND
AND FEEL THE SUN.

CLOSE IT

AND YOU CAN'T CATCH ANY LIGHT

INSIDE.

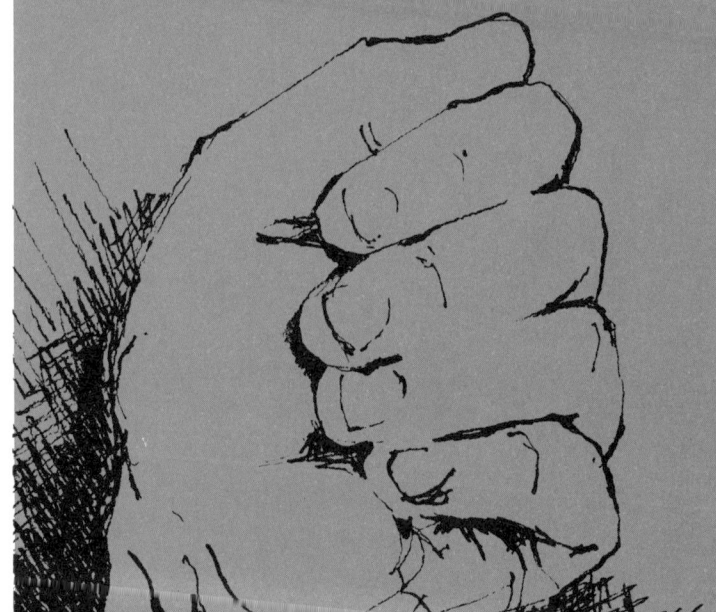

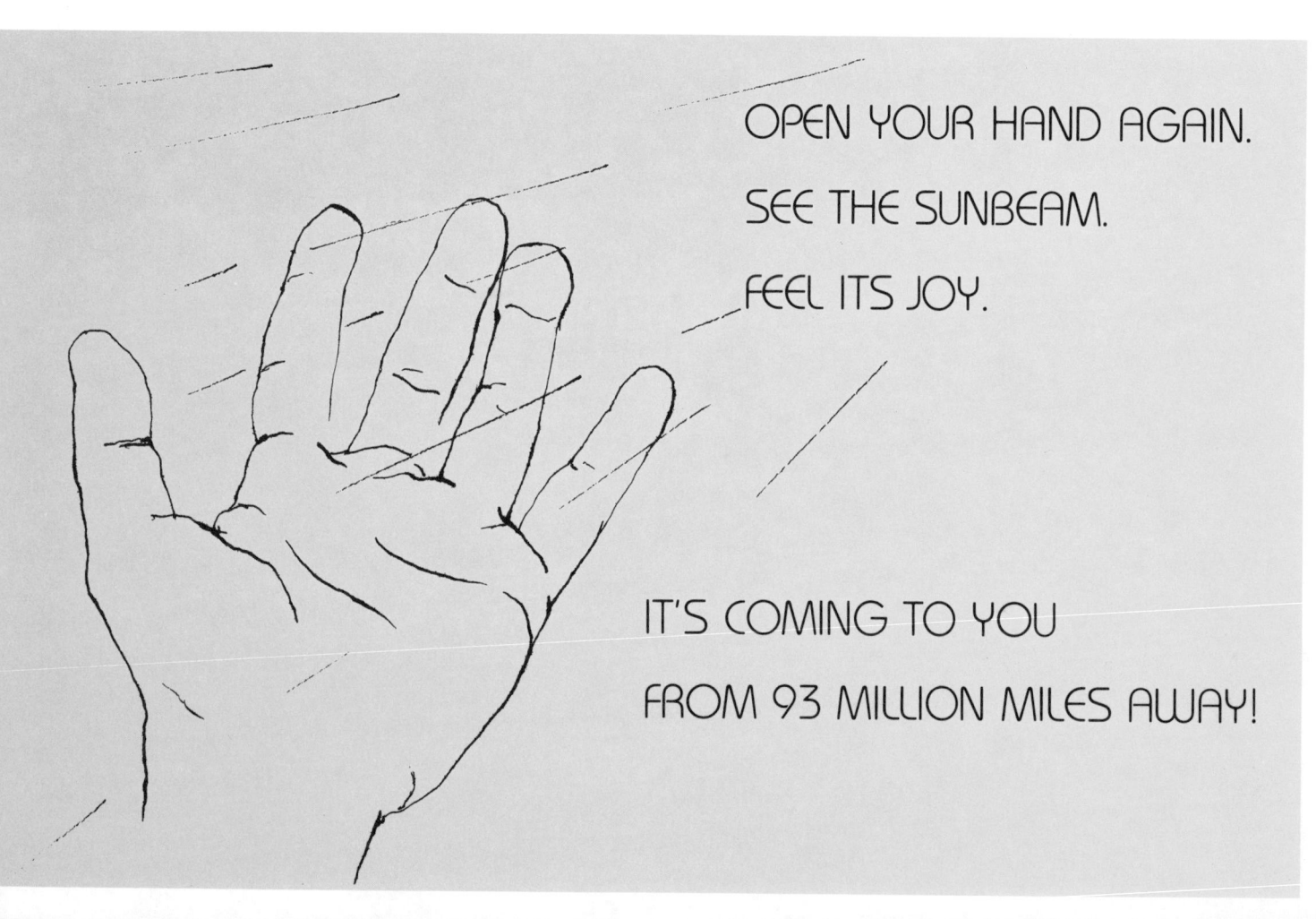

THIS BEAM IS HERE, AND YET

IT'S NEVER APART FROM ITS SUN...

LIKE YOU

LIKE YOU

LIKE YOU...

CLOSE YOUR EYES.

IT'S DARK...

WHERE DID THE SUN GO?